AA

is for

AARDVARK

By Mark Shulman

Illustrated by Tamara Petrosino

Sterling Publishing Co., Inc.

New York

Printed in China

Library of Congress Cataloging-in-Publication Data Available

10 9 8 7 6 5 4 3 2 1

Published by Sterling Publishing Co., Inc.
387 Park Avenue South, New York, NY 10016
Text © 2005 by Mark Shulman
Illustrations © 2005 by Tamara Petrosino
Designed by Nicky Lindeman

Created at Oomf, Inc.
www.Oomf.com

Distributed in Canada by Sterling Publishing
c/o Canadian Manda Group, 165 Dufferin Street
Toronto, Ontario, Canada M6K 3H6
Distributed in Great Britain and Europe by Chris Lloyd at Orca Book
Services, Stanley House, Fleets Lane, Poole BH15 3AJ, England
Distributed in Australia by Capricorn Link (Australia) Pty. Ltd.
P.O. Box 704, Windsor, NSW 2756, Australia

Printed in China
Sterling ISBN 1-4027-2871-9

For information about custom editions, special sales, premium and
corporate purchases, please contact Sterling Special Sales
Department at 800-805-5489 or specialsales@sterlingpub.com.

For S.S., who is an AA++ boy.   — MS

To my Grandma, Grandpa, Nanny, and Pop Pop, in loving memory.   — TP

Special thanks to Frances, Charlie, and Nicky.

And to David W. at MusicForAardvarks.com, for the groovy background music.

A A

is for

AARDVARK

BB is for rubber band.

cc is for raccoon.

EE is for beep! beep!

Gg is for egg salad.

HH is for shh!

II is for Hawaii.

JJ is for 2 jacks.

KK is for trekking (while knockkneed).

LL is for a frilly yellow pillow.

MM is for yummy.

NN is for bunny.

oo is for toodle-oo!

PP is for hippo. A happy, hippie hippo.

QQ is for 2 queens.

(Hey, it worked for the jacks!)

RR is for furry . . . and hurry!

SS is for pussycat.

This one doesn't like the wilderness!

TT is for a safe little kitten.

Uu is for vacuum.

VV is for skivvies.

XX is for six xylophone players, and one ex-xylophone player.

YY is for a very young ant.

ZZ is for puzzles.

Just what an aardvark loves to play!